G
CEN   ...ning

Novels for Students, Volume 43

Project Editor: Sara Constantakis Rights Acquisition and Management: Robyn Young Composition: Evi Abou-El-Seoud Manufacturing: Rhonda Dover

Imaging: John Watkins

Product Design: Pamela A. E. Galbreath, Jennifer Wahi Digital Content Production: Allie Semperger Product Manager: Meggin Condino © 2013 Gale, Cengage Learning

ALL RIGHTS RESERVED. No part of this work covered by the copyright herein may be reproduced, transmitted, stored, or used in any form or by any means graphic, electronic, or mechanical, including but not limited to photocopying, recording, scanning, digitizing, taping, Web distribution, information networks, or information storage and retrieval systems, except as permitted under Section 107 or 108 of the 1976 United States Copyright Act, without the prior written permission of the publisher.

Since this page cannot legibly accommodate all copyright notices, the acknowledgments constitute an extension of the copyright notice.

For product information and technology assistance, contact us at **Gale Customer Support, 1-800-877-4253.**

For permission to use material from this text or product, submit all requests online at **www.cengage.com/permissions**.

Further permissions questions can be e-mailed to **permissionrequest@cengage.com** While every effort has been made to ensure the reliability of the information presented in this publication, Gale, a part of Cengage Learning, does not guarantee the accuracy of the data contained herein. Gale accepts no payment for listing; and inclusion in the publication of any organization, agency, institution, publication, service, or individual does not imply endorsement of the editors or publisher. Errors brought to the attention of the publisher and verified to the satisfaction of the publisher will be corrected in future editions.

Gale
27500 Drake Rd.
Farmington Hills, MI, 48331-3535

ISBN-13: 978-1-4144-9486-9
ISBN-10: 1-4144-9486-6
ISSN 1094-3552

This title is also available as an e-book.

ISBN-13: 978-1-4144-9272-8
ISBN-10: 1-4144-9272-3
Contact your Gale, a part of Cengage Learning sales
representative for ordering information.

Printed in Mexico
1 2 3 4 5 6 7 17 16 15 14 13

Mother to Mother

Sindiwe Magona 1998

Introduction

Published in South Africa in 1998 and in the United States in 1999, Sindiwe Magona's fictional work, *Mother to Mother*, is based on the 1993 murder of Amy Biehl, an American student who was helping organize democratic elections in South Africa. The story is told from the perspective of Mandisa, a mother whose son participated in the murder. She writes a letter both to encourage Amy's mother, Mrs. Biehl, and to explain the culture that killed her daughter. This epistolary novel explores the effects of apartheid in South Africa. The themes of racism and hatred blend with the love and sorrow of motherhood in this story of loss and attempted reconciliation.

Author Biography

Magona was born on August 27, 1943, in Gungululu in Transkei, which is near Tsolo. Magona's family moved to Cape Town when she was four so her father could find work. She describes a nomadic childhood in her autobiography, *Forced to Grow*. "And there we had lived, moving from one segregated residential area to another until, in 1960, we were moved." The family was finally settled in the township of Guguletu. Despite the social injustice of apartheid, she was able to complete her secondary education and undergraduate studies from the University of South Africa by correspondence.

Magona worked as a teacher when she was nineteen, but she was forced to leave when she became pregnant. She married Luthando and worked in service jobs for wealthy white families until Luthando told her employer that he would no longer allow it. Her husband abandoned his family when Magona was twenty-three and pregnant with their third child. Magona again worked in domestic service to provide for her family while taking night courses, and she eventually returned to teaching. In 1981, she moved to New York City, where she attended Columbia University on a scholarship to earn a master's degree in social work.

After completing her education in 1983, Magona returned to her family in South Africa. She took a job at the United Nations in New York in 1984, where she worked toward ending apartheid by hosting radio programs until the rise of democracy in South Africa in 1994. In 1990, she published her first autobiography, To *My Children's Children. Forced to Grow*, another autobiography, soon followed in 1992. In 1993, she was granted an honorary doctorate by Hartwick College. *Mother to Mother* was published in 1998 on the five-year anniversary of Amy Biehl's murder, at the request of the Biehl family.

Magona retired from the United Nations and returned to South Africa in 2003. She continues to write while she works to promote a safe and just society in South Africa. Her other works include poetry, essays, plays, translations, and children's books. Magona has earned numerous awards, such as the Molteno Gold Medal for Lifetime Achievement and the Xhosa Heroes Award. In 2011, South African president Jacob G. Zuma presented her with the Order of Ikhamanga in Bronze.

Plot Summary

Chapter 1: Mandisa's Lament

Mother to Mother is an epistolary novel—taking the form of letters from one character to another—based on the 1993 murder of American Fulbright scholar Amy Biehl in South Africa. It is a letter to Biehl's mother from the mother of the teenage boy convicted of killing her. Magona includes words and phrases in the Xhosa language throughout the book, but they are either translated or clear from their context.

The first chapter is printed in italics because it directly addresses Mrs. Biehl. Mandisa introduces herself with the words: "My son killed your daughter." She goes on to explain that people blame her for the murder, assuming that she could control his actions. Mandisa, however, could not restrain her son. Even his conception was beyond her control; it was an event that she believes ruined her life.

Mandisa does say that she is not surprised her son committed murder because he is one of "these monsters our children have become." She is surprised, however, that Amy, a white woman, chose to come to Guguletu, an all-black reservation, or homeland, where she would be in danger. Here Mandisa contrasts the difference between her son and Amy. Amy did not realize her danger because her own experiences and good nature led her to believe that other people are good. Mandisa's son, on the other hand, knew only injustice, poverty, and violence. Now the government does more to protect his life than it did before he became a murderer. Mandisa ends the chapter by expressing her shame at her son's actions, confessing her love for him and asking God to forgive him.

Chapter 2: Mowbray—Wednesday 25 August 1993

The second chapter does not use italics because Mandisa shares what she imagines and experienced instead of addressing Mrs. Biehl directly. She begins by imagining Amy eating breakfast in a comfortable apartment before driving to the university. At the same time, Mandisa is waking her teenage children. Her daughter, Siziwe, has a room, but the boys, Mxolisi and Lunga, sleep in a tin hut, or *hokkie*, behind the house because the government-issued houses are too small for a family. She suppresses guilt at leaving her children alone while she works all day in the home of a white woman. She comes home too late and tired to keep her children in line. Mandisa knows that her family cannot survive without her job, but she also realizes that her absence creates another problem.

Mandisa shifts to a scene in which Amy says goodbye to her friends at the university. Amy is torn between happiness at the thought of going home and the sadness of leaving her friends. The rest of the chapter transitions quickly between the victim and her killer. Mxolisi, Mandisa's older son, does not go to school because of boycotts to protest the government. Instead he meets his friends in the street. At the university, Amy offers to drive her friends home to Guguletu. Meanwhile, Mxolisi and his friends vandalize a truck and chant political slogans as Amy's car approaches. They stone the car and kill the driver when they see that she is white.

Chapter 3: 5:15 p.m.—Wednesday 25 August 1993

Mandisa is working when her employer returns early and tells her that she has to go home because there is trouble in Guguletu. The employer drives Mandisa to the station because white people are not allowed in the district of Guguletu. The people on the bus speculate about what happened in their district. Mandisa considers the fact that there has been violence in the districts since the 1976 Soweto riots and the rise of student protests against apartheid.

She has a flashback to the time she came to Guguletu as a child. The district was already overcrowded and filled with broken families looking for their relatives. When Mandisa gets off the bus, she is nearly trampled by the police and other travelers. She loses a shoe and cuts her foot, but her primary concern is for her children, particularly Siziwe, as she makes her way home.

Chapter 4: 7:30 p.m.

Siziwe meets Mandisa when she arrives at the house. Lunga is home, but Mxolisi is not there. Mandisa is annoyed because she knows that Siziwe is hiding something from her. Her husband, Dwadwa, is not home either, but her main concern is for Mxolisi.

7:45 P.M.

Skonana, Mandisa's neighbor, comes over. She informs Mandisa that a white woman was stabbed on their street. Mandisa knows that the police, who do nothing to stop violence in Guguletu, will investigate this murder because the victim was white. The police are known to torture and kill innocent people in Guguletu, and she is afraid.

Chapter 5

Mandisa asks herself why anyone would come to Guguletu. She recalls how, as a girl, she came to the township in a "dispersal of the government's making.... More than three decades later, my people are still reeling from it." She has another flashback to the time when she was nine years old. People in her village, Blouvlei, hear rumors that the government will remove all black people from their land, but no one believes it is possible. She remembers a happy home with her brother and parents, where her mother greets them every day after school. *Mama* is a term used for all older women, and *tata* means "father."

The next year, flyers are dropped from planes, informing the people that they have one month to relocate. Three months later, they are forcibly moved in the middle of the night as their homes are demolished. When the family comes to Guguletu, both parents have to work full-time for them to survive. She believes that "everything and everybody changed."

10:05 P.M.—WEDNESDAY 25 AUGUST 1993

Mxolisi and Dwadwa are still not home. Mandisa is concerned about her son and wonders why he stopped confiding in her. Dwadwa returns, and Mandisa cooks the spleen he brings home for the family supper. She considers how fortunate they are to have meat more than once a week.

Mandisa thinks about other times the help of white people was rejected; she recalls when three white nurses were attacked in 1960. After arguing with Dwadwa about Mxolisi's choice to abandon school and wander the streets, Mandisa reveals her belief that the education system failed and her children now suffer because of this failure.

In a section of the text that is in italics, she asks Mrs. Biehl whether her daughter went to school, and why she came to Guguletu if she was educated. She returns to describe the change that came over the children after school was rejected. At first, they burned down schools and stoned the cars of white people. This led to violence against members of their own community who were seen as traitors. The children became more difficult to control, but they were praised for their actions.

Chapter 6: 4:00 a.m.—Thursday 26 August 1993

Mandisa is awake in her bedroom when the police storm in to search for Mxolisi. The family is terrified, particularly Siziwe. Mandisa is questioned and slapped, and the *hokkie* is torn apart. Unable to find Mxolisi, the white police officers beat Lunga before leaving.

Chapter 7

The chapter begins by repeating an italicized statement from the first chapter, saying that Mxolisi was always trouble. Mandisa describes his conception as an event "totally destroying the me I was. The me I would have become." The chapter transitions from italics to a flashback of the circumstances surrounding Mxolisi's birth in 1973, when Mandisa was fifteen.

At the age of thirteen, Mandisa's mother panics that the teenager will "get a stomach," or become pregnant. Mandisa is not allowed to spend time with boys, but she meets China in school and becomes his girlfriend. Her mother becomes even more protective of her daughter's virginity when she learns that her son, Khaya, is dating Mandisa's now-pregnant friend Nono. She sends Mandisa away to live with her grandmother in Gungululu.

GUNGULULU—SEPTEMBER 1972

In Gungululu, Mandisa finishes primary school and is ranked second in her class. When Mandisa learns that her aunt is coming from the South African city of East London to have her baby, she plans on asking to accompany her home to East London so she can continue her education. Mandisa's dreams are shattered, however, when her aunt and grandmother notice that she is pregnant. Mandisa is confused because she is still technically a virgin. She cannot believe that she is three months pregnant. Her mother is contacted and brings Mandisa home in disgrace.

Chapter 8

In italics, Mandisa expresses the shame that Mxolisi brought her. His birth was a shame to her family.

During the ride home, the driver rants against the wealthy settlers who stole their land. When she arrives in Guguletu, Mandisa is not allowed to leave the house. She manages to contact China, but he refuses to take responsibility for the baby. Her family brings the case before China's clan, but they are slow to respond. A priest insists that they marry, and the clans begin negotiating.

Mandisa is still unmarried when her son is born, and she names him Hlumelo. Mandisa no longer wishes to marry China after the birth of her son; she wants to continue her education. Her clan, however, demands that her father make Mandisa go through with the marriage to China once the details are arranged. A few months after her son is born, Mandisa is married when the families exchange a dowry and bride price, or *lobola*. She becomes part of a new clan. According to tradition, she is renamed, and the grandparents name her son. She is given a mocking name, and her son is renamed Mxolisi, meaning "he who would bring peace."

Her marriage is unhappy. As the newest wife, Mandisa must serve the rest of the family while caring for her son. She begins losing weight, and China's family refuses to fulfill their promise to allow her to go to school. Shortly after Mxolisi turns two, China disappears. Mandisa, who is left without any financial support, goes to work as a domestic servant. Soon she has the money to rent a *hokkie* and live on her own. Unfortunately, the changes affect her son, who misses his other relatives.

Mxolisi enjoys playing with the teenage boys of the family who rent Mandisa her *hokkie*. Zuzi and Mzamo treat Mxolisi like a brother. One day, the police chase Zuzi and Mzamo home, where they hide in a closet. Mxolisi tells the police where his friends are hiding, and he is traumatized when the boys are shot in front of him. Mxolisi does not speak after this incident. China's father intervenes and takes them to a healer, or *sangomo*. She tells Mandisa to free Mxolisi from her resentment of him. Mandisa knows that the *sangomo* is correct, and she tries to stop resenting her son for the life his birth took away from her.

Shortly after this meeting, Mandisa goes to her brother's wedding, where she meets Lungile. She refuses to marry him, but she allows him to stay with her as long as he wants. Lunga is born within a year. Mxolisi begins to wet his bed after the birth of his brother. After being punished, he asks, "Where is my own father?" These are the first words he has spoken in two years, and Mandisa has no answer.

Mxolisi is a bright student when he begins school. He starts to hate school, however, when teachers beat him for not having the money for fees. Meanwhile, Lungile leaves to become a freedom fighter. Mandisa persuades Mxolisi to stay in school, but he chooses to boycott classes in high school after becoming involved in politics. By this time, Mandisa has married Dwadwa, and Siziwe has been born.

Instead of going to school, Mxolisi roams the streets with his friends protesting and chanting slogans such as "One settler! One bullet!" Mandisa's neighbors, however, tell her she should be proud of Mxolisi. He has a good reputation in the community. In fact, he saved a girl from being raped when no one else would intervene. Now the same people who praised Mxolisi scorn Mandisa.

Chapter 9

6 A.M.—THURSDAY 26 AUGUST

Mandisa returns the narrative to the morning after the murder. After the police leave, her neighbors come over, but Dwadwa chases them away. Lunga is beaten, but the wounds are superficial. Siziwe is traumatized, and she tells her mother that Mxolisi came home and left quickly before Mandisa arrived. Mandisa wonders why the police want Mxolisi, and Dwadwa tells her, "How long have I told you that this child will bring us heavy trouble one day?" He leaves for work, and Mandisa falls asleep.

Chapter 10

Mandisa has another flashback to her childhood. She remembers when her grandfather Tatomkhulu came to live with her family. From him, she learns the history of South Africa from the perspective of the native people. He begins, "For, let me tell you something, deep run the roots of hatred here." He explains that the white settlers came and took their land. To be rid of the settlers, the Xhosa people sacrificed all of their cattle and crops because the prophet Nongqawause promised that the land would be restored and the settlers driven away. The prophecy is printed in italics, emphasizing the importance of this oral history. The sacrifice was unsuccessful, and the people were forced to work in the mines or starve. The same hatred that motivated the sacrifice motivates Mxolisi's actions.

1 P.M.—THURSDAY 26 AUGUST

Siziwe wakes Mandisa and tells her that Lunga has gone with some boys. Siziwe also tells her that she believes Mxolisi had something to do with the murder. Mandisa does not have time to process this information before Reverend Mananga comes to the house. He leaves a message that Mxolisi's group may use the church to meet, and he gives Mandisa a note with instructions to take a taxi to the last stop. There, she is given instructions to go to a location where a car takes her to Mxolisi's hiding place.

Mandisa asks Mxolisi if he killed the girl, and he swears that he was not the only one to attack the car and was not the only one to stab her. Mandisa is both angry and terrified. She lashes out at the stupidity of killing a white woman and sees the fear in her son's eyes. They cling to each other and cry, and she finds herself unable to release his hand.

Chapter 11

Returning to italics, Mandisa questions her "Sister-Mother," asking what she should do with her son. She wonders if they are enemies and if caring for her son means that she does not mourn the death of the girl he murdered. She also wishes that Amy had known fear and stayed away from Guguletu.

Leaving italics, she says that the same people who praised her son now treat her family with derision. Although Mandisa is ashamed of what Mxolisi has done, she places some of the blame on the leaders who encouraged his behavior, saying, "They, as surely as my son, are your daughter's murderers." Mandisa sees no changes from the children in her community or the leaders who encourage them. She asks why her son was the only one punished for a mob attack, and she ends the chapter mourning the actions of her son and asking for God's help.

GUGULETU, MUCH LATER

Mandisa's friends and neighbors come to help her grieve. With their help, she is able to find strength and hope for the future. The knowledge that people are helping children in Guguletu gives her hope that violence will end. She also allows herself to hope that Mxolisi will find a better life. She ends the chapter in italics, attempting to console her Sister-Mother, telling her that she has nothing to be ashamed of in the way that she raised her child.

Chapter 12

In italics, Mandisa restates a question from the first chapter. "What had he to live for?" He saw his future in the lives of the men around him, who worked labor-intensive jobs with little pay. There are no chances for anyone to advance who is born outside the "white world." Mandisa believes his generation is lost because they see only despair for the future.

GUGULETU—LATE AFTERNOON, WEDNESDAY 25 AUGUST

The final chapter of the books plays out the events of the murder from the moment Amy's car enters Guguletu. Mandisa calls her son the "sharpened arrow of the wrath of his race" while Amy was "the sacrifice of hers." She ends by wishing that circumstances had been different and her son would not yet be a murderer, which implies that the hatred necessary to kill would always be with him.

Amy Biehl

Mandisa does not use Amy Biehl's name, but the character is clearly Amy from the introduction. A Fulbright scholar, Amy was assisting with the first democratic election in South Africa. Mandisa imagines her last day in detail. In Mandisa's mind, she spends the day saying goodbye to her friends because she will soon return to the United States. She drives her friends home to Guguletu, where she is murdered. In the real history, a group of boys in Guguletu were convicted of her murder. In the fictionalized version in this book, Mxolisi is the only one convicted of murdering Amy.

Mrs. Biehl

Mandisa does not call her "Sister-Mother" by name, but the letter is obviously addressed to Amy's mother. She is Mandisa's audience, and the reader must speculate on her reaction to the letter.

China

China is Mandisa's first boyfriend and, later, her husband. He resents Mandisa for not having an abortion. Bitter about being forced to marry Mandisa, he abandons his family after Mxolisi's second birthday.

Dwadwa

Dwadwa is Mandisa's second husband and Siziwe's father. He warns Mandisa that Mxolisi will cause them trouble.

Funiwe

Funiwe is Mandisa's aunt. She lives in East London, but she travels to Gungululu to be with her mother when she is pregnant.

Hlumelo

See Mxolisi

Khaya

Khaya is Mandisa's brother. He dates Mandisa's best friend, Nono, when they are teenagers. Nono becomes pregnant, which causes Mandisa's mother to grow even stricter with Mandisa. Khaya marries Nono when she is pregnant with their second child.

Kukwana

Kukwana is the childhood name of Mandisa and Khaya's mother. She works a service job to provide for her family after moving to Guguletu. She is overprotective of Mandisa and sends her away after she learns Nono is pregnant. She is humiliated when she discovers that Mandisa is pregnant.

Lunga

Lunga is the son of Mandisa and Lungile. His parents are never married, and his father leaves to become a freedom fighter. The police beat him because he is Mxolisi's brother.

Lungile

Lungile meets Mandisa at Nono and Khaya's wedding. He is the father of Lunga, but he leaves Mandisa to become a freedom fighter.

Makhulu

Makhulu is Mandisa's grandmother. Mandisa discovers that she is pregnant while staying with Makhulu in Gungululu.

Reverend Mananga

Reverend Mananga is a friend of Mxolisi's who come to Mandisa's home the day after the murder. Pretending to leave a message for Mxolisi, he secretly slips a note to Mandisa. The note provides instructions that take her to Mxolisi's hiding place.

Mandisa

Mandisa is Mxolisi's mother and the narrator of *Mother to Mother*. She feels conflicted between feelings of love for her son and shame that he murdered Amy Biehl. In an effort to comfort Mrs. Biehl, she writes a letter sharing details about her feelings, her life, and society under apartheid. Her private confessions explore the history of race relations in South Africa as well as the changes that apartheid brought to society.

Mandisa uses flashbacks to her own childhood and Mxolisi's childhood to explain life in Guguletu. As a child, she is relocated from her home to Guguletu. She finds herself pregnant with Mxolisi as a teenager, and she is both a wife and mother at the age of fifteen. Mandisa works in service jobs to provide for her family after her husband abandons her. She has a relationship with Lungile and gives birth to her second son, Lunga. After Lungile leaves, she marries Dwadwa and has her daughter, Siziwe.

Mandisa feels guilty that work prevents her from spending more time with her children, but she must work for her family to survive. After the murder, she suffers the rejection of her peers. After her neighbors reach out to her, she becomes hopeful that the future will be better.

Mxolisi

Mxolisi is the son of Mandisa and China.

Mandisa names him Hlumelo, but his father's family renames him Mxolisi, meaning "he who would bring peace." China abandons him when he is two, and Mandisa raises him on her own. Shortly after his father leaves, Mxolisi innocently informs the police where two of his friends are hiding. He is traumatized when they are killed in front him, and he does not speak for two years.

As a teenager, Mxolisi boycotts school as a political protest. He saves a girl from being raped when no one else will help her. This noble act brings him respect in Guguletu, but the respect is short-lived. Filled with rage at white oppression, he participates in the murder of Amy Biehl simply because she is a white person in Guguletu. He hides, but he is discovered by the police and convicted of murder.

Mzamo

Mzamo is the teenage son of Mandisa's landlord. He and his brother, Zuzi, play with Mxolisi when he is a young child. The police kill him when Mxolisi innocently tells them where he and Zuzi are hiding.

Nongqawause

Nongqawause is the prophet who advised the Xhosa people to sacrifice all of their crops and cattle. She promised that the sacrifice would drive the settlers away and save their land. The prophecy is unfulfilled, and the people suffer starvation because of their sacrifice.

Nono

Nono is Mandisa's best friend. She dates Khaya, Mandisa's brother and becomes pregnant as a teenager. She marries Khaya when she is pregnant with their second child.

Sister-Mother

See Mrs. Biehl

Siziwe

Siziwe is Mandisa's youngest child and her only daughter. Siziwe's father is Dwadwa. She initially hides information about Mxolisi from Mandisa. After the police leave their house, she is traumatized and tells her mother that Mxolisi came home after the murder but left the house before Mandisa arrived.

Skonana

Skonana is Mandisa's neighbor. She comes over the night of the murder and tells Mandisa that a white girl was stabbed on their street that day. Long after the murder, she comes to help Mandisa grieve.

Tatomkhulu

Tatomkhulu is Mandisa's grandfather. He teaches her history from the perspective of the Xhosa people. He explains that hatred is part of South African history and culture. He tells her hatred for white settlers was the reason why the Xhosa people were willing to accept Nongqawause's prophecy and sacrifice their crops and cattle.

Zuzi

Zuzi is the teenage son of Mandisa's landlord. He and his brother, Mzamo, play with Mxolisi when he is a young child. The police kill him when Mxolisi innocently tells them where he and Mzamo are hiding.

Themes

Hatred

The theme of hatred appears throughout *Mother to Mother*. As a child, Mandisa learns that "deep run the roots of hatred here." The hostility that arises when settlers first come to South Africa only grows with each injustice. Over time, this turns into a legacy of hatred. Mandisa's grandfather tells her about the time when the Xhosa people were willing to risk everything to remove the hated settlers from their land. After their sacrifice fails, the settlers continue to take more and more from the native peoples. The Xhosa people and other natives are left with poverty and little hope. All they have is their hatred.

As a community, people in Guguletu refer to white people as "white dogs." Their children grow up hearing this anger and are encouraged to take back power from the people who stole their land. The chant "One settler! One bullet!" shows the depth of their rage. Unfortunately, the result of the children's hatred is violence that tears apart their own community. Mandisa describes the social decline as children move from destroying the property of white individuals to attacking and killing people in Guguletu accused of collaboration.

The murder of a white American student is fueled by blind rage at a perceived oppressor.

Mxolisi has no idea that she is a foreigner attempting to help his cause. Mxolisi does not act rationally. He embodies generations of hatred born from injustice that goes back centuries. As Mandisa explains, "My son was only an agent, executing the long-simmering dark desires of his race."

Topics for Further Study

- Research Amy Biehl's parents and their reaction to their daughter's murder. Write a letter in the voice of Mrs. Biehl responding to Mandisa's letter in *Mother to Mother*. Knowing what you do about the family, how do you think she would react to Mandisa? Would she be able to forgive Mxolisi and Mandisa? Share your letter in front of the class and discuss the reasons for your response.

- Read *Climbing the Stairs*, by Padma Venkatraman. This young-adult book tells the story of Vidya, a teenage girl who lives in India under British occupation. She hopes to go to college, but her life is forever altered after her father is injured in a riot and suffers brain damage. Create mockups of social network pages (such as Twitter, Facebook, Myspace, Google+) for Mandisa and Vidya. What experiences do they share? How could Mandisa encourage Vidya?

- Research the history of apartheid in South Africa. Create a web page that includes links to influential laws, events, and individuals over the decades. Be sure to include a link to a biographical time line of Sindiwe Magona. You may also include links to personal stories of people affected by apartheid.

- Read *Forced to Grow*, by Sindiwe Magona. This autobiography shares her struggle to provide for her family under apartheid. Write a paper that compares and contrasts her experiences with Mandisa's. In what ways are their lives similar, and in what ways are they different? Why do you think Magona was finally able to continue her education and Mandisa was not?

- Research the life of Amy Biehl, beginning with the Amy Biehl Foundation. Write a one-act play in which Amy's spirit visits Mxolisi in prison. What do you think she would say to him? How do you think he would he react to her? Perform the play with a friend and record it. Upload the performance to a blog or website.

Racism

The Anti-Defamation League defines *racism* as the "hatred of one person by another—or the belief that another person is less than human—because of skin color, language, customs, [or] place of birth." Racism motivates the injustice and hatred that are described in *Mother to Mother*. The belief that the native peoples of South African people are inferior is used to justify taking their land and, eventually, to impose apartheid, the official policy of racial segregation. The racism that Mandisa and her family experience on a daily basis is exposed when the police, who are mainly white, come searching for Mxolisi and harass his family. The police do not take action to protect the inhabitants of Guguletu, and the people live with constant violence. In fact, the police are often the cause of violence. For example, the police beat Lunga for no reason and one officer says, "We are tired of this ... of you people."

Racism takes away the hope of people outside white society, creating a festering resentment against the "white dogs" who took their land. Mxolisi attacks a girl simply because she is white. When he looks at her, all he sees is another white oppressor. Political leaders encourage racism and hatred, and Mandisa places some of the blame for her son's actions on them. As she tells her "Sister-Mother": "They knew, or should have known, better. They were adults. They were learned. They had key to reason."

Motherhood

Mandisa is able to sympathize with the loss and pain that Amy's mother feels because she suffers a similar loss. Motherhood and tragedy bind the two women together. Mandisa knows that, as a mother, Mrs. Biehl can understand the complex emotions that she feels. Mandisa grieves for her own loss and for Mrs. Biehl's; both of them have lost their children. Mandisa shifts between her own sense of anger, shame, love, and grief throughout the book.

Mandisa is ashamed of her son for killing another person. She is ashamed of herself because she leaves her children alone in Guguletu to work in a white household. She feels anger at the society that forces her to work away from her children in order for her family to survive. She grieves that other children live the same life as her son, and she is concerned about their futures. She feels that they are becoming monsters. "Does anyone see this? Do their mothers see this? Did I see it?"

Mandisa is quick to admit her shortcomings as a mother, particularly in her treatment of Mxolisi. Her feelings for Mxolisi have always been complicated. While pregnant, she feels only bitterness toward him, but this becomes love once he is born. Subconsciously, however, she still resents him for, as she puts it, "destroying the me I was." Still, she defends Mxolisi against her husband's assertions that he will bring trouble, loving him with the unconditional love of a mother.

Mandisa contrasts her perceived failure as a mother with what she assumes are the successes of Mrs. Biehl, who was able to give her daughter the opportunities and attention that Mandisa never could. They both mourn the loss of children, but that is through no fault of Mrs. Biehl'. Mandisa attempts to encourage Mrs. Biehl by pointing out that she was a good mother. "But you, remember this, let it console you some, you never have to ask yourself: What did I not do for this child?"

Epistolary Novel

Mother to Mother is an epistolary novel. According to William Harmon in *A Handbook to Literature*, an epistolary novel is "a novel in which the narrative is carried forward by letters written by one or more of the characters." By creating a fictional letter from the mother of a murderer to the mother of the girl he killed, Magona allows the readers to glimpse Mandisa's conflicted feelings regarding her son. *Mother to Mother* does not use a traditional epistle style. It does not include a salutation or signature. She introduces the letter with the words "My son killed your daughter." Over the course of the book, Mandisa addresses Mrs. Biehl as "Sister-Mother." The book is a single letter, written to connect with and console Amy Biehl's mother. It also sheds light on the history of the South Africa and the legacy of apartheid. Magona allows the readers to imagine how the letter is received.

Confession

Magona weaves elements of a confession into her epistle. According to Harmon, a confession is "a form of autobiography that deals with customarily hidden or highly private matters." In the letter, Mandisa tells her life story and Mxolisi's life story in the context of apartheid. Her personal feelings and reactions to deeply personal situations are exposed for Mrs. Biehl to read. For example, she confesses her feelings of resentment toward Mxolisi for taking away the life she could have had. She also admits that her shame for Mxolisi's crime is mixed with overwhelming love for her child.

Flashback

The story of *Mother to Mother* is not told in linear order but instead relies on flashbacks, which show events that occurred before the time frame of the novel. The book opens after the murder of Amy Biehl, and the narrative primarily occurs over two days, the day of the murder and the next day. Mandisa uses flashbacks, however, to share stories from her past throughout her letter, such as when, as a child, she was forced to move from her village to Guguletu. She also describes falling in love with China, giving birth to Mxolisi, and her unhappy marriage. These past events shed light on the present.

European Settlement of South Africa

The history of European settlers in South Africa plays an important role in race relations and Mandisa's story in *Mother to Mother*. The Dutch first arrived in South Africa in 1652, when Jan van Riebeeck landed at the Cape of Good Hope. They bartered with the native Khoekhoe people, but tension developed when the European settlers were seen as a threat. In 1657, slaves were imported to work farmland given to Jan van Riebeeck's men for their service. By 1662, there were two hundred fifty Europeans living in South Africa.

In the 1700s, European settlers, called *trekboers*, were encouraged to travel to South Africa. Once there, the settlers began to claim land that belonged to the native people. These settlers included people from Holland, France, and Germany. In 1792, the Cape of Good Hope came under British rule. It changed hands between the Dutch, British, and French several times over the years because of the Napoleonic Wars. By the second half of the century, the settlers had traveled to land occupied by the Xhosa people.

The British began the Cape Frontier Wars against the Xhosa people in 1820. The Xhosa people resisted the influx of settlers coming to take their land. This struggle ended in 1857 "with the mass starvation" of the people, as South-Africa.info notes. The people starved because of a failed prophecy. The Xhosa people were willing to slaughter their cattle and destroy their crops based on a prophecy that promised the sacrifice would drive the European settlers back to the ocean. This moment in history is important to the plot of *Mother to Mother*.

Apartheid

Apartheid officially began in 1948, when the Nationalist Party took control of the government. In 1950, the Population Registration Act divided the population into three different races: white, black/African, and colored/mixed. The colored category included people of mixed ancestry or individuals who were neither white nor African. The law also made interracial marriage illegal.

Compare & Contrast

- **1990s:** Apartheid laws, which oppress a majority of the population of South Africa, are in effect when Frederik Willem de Klerk becomes president in 1990. He begins loosening restrictions and repealing apartheid laws. The election of Nelson Mandela in 1994 is the result of the nation's first democratic election.

Today: Apartheid laws have been abolished. South Africa is a republic with universal suffrage, and everyone, regardless of race, has the right to elect government officials. While it is true that racism still exists, the government no longer protects it.

- **1990s:** Limitations on education and unequal pay keep citizens who are not white from improving economically. Because of decades of apartheid laws, most people in South Africa live in poverty.

  Today: The country has improved economically, but it is still struggling to fix the damage created by apartheid. As the *CIA: World Fact Book* points out, "Daunting economic problems remain from the apartheid era—especially poverty, lack of economic empowerment among the disadvantaged groups, and a shortage of public transportation." Half of the nation lives below the poverty line.

- **1990s:** As the nation begins to shift away from apartheid, violence dominates South Africa. Political protests grow violent, and the

government reacts brutally. Additionally, there is a high crime rate within the black community.
Today: Crime rates within South Africa remain high. Racially motivated violence still occurs. Recent reports from the South African Police Service, however, show an overall decline in crime.

The following year, the Bantu Homelands Act allotted specific land to Africans. The homelands, similar to reservations, operated as separate nations, meaning that the inhabitants were no longer considered citizens of South Africa. Leaving the homelands required passports, and many people worked service jobs for white households, which forced them to travel beyond their homelands. Over the years, people were forcibly moved from their land and homes to four homelands, which were too small to support all of the inhabitants. These relocations were traumatic. As Bradley Skelcher points out in an article in the *Journal of Black Studies*, the people "who were not at their homesteads when the trucks came, were left behind, forcing them to wander by foot in search of their families."

In 1953, nonwhites were prohibited from attending universities, and all education came under white government control. The Public Safety Act and the Criminal Law Amendment Act enacted the same year allowed the government to declare a state of emergency for any protest against apartheid laws. People could be beaten, whipped, or jailed without trial. Protests were met with violent opposition, such as the Sharpeville protest in 1960, where sixty-nine people were killed after refusing to carry their passes. Resistance increased in 1970s, spurred by the South African Students Organization.

International pressure and internal protest brought changes in the 1990s. In 1990, President de Klerk lifted restrictions on opposition groups and began dismantling apartheid laws. Violence, however, continued to dominate the nation despite political negotiation. The first democratic elections were seen as a sign that apartheid was finally being ended. The elections were held from April 26 to April 28, 1994, and Nelson Mandela was sworn in as president on May 10, 1994.

Critical Overview

Criticism of Magona's writing has been positive. Her first two books, *To My Children's Children and Forced to Grow*, are autobiographies, and critics praised her honesty, insight, and explanation of Xhosa culture. For example, the *Publisher's Weekly* review of *To My Children's Children* notes, "Her vivid descriptions of Xhosa customs unfold not as an anthropologist's field study but as a memory etched from experience." Likewise, Ann Burns praised Magona's writing style in her review of *Forced to Grow for the Library Journal*. She does say, however, that "a pronunciation guide would have been helpful for African languages."

Mother to Mother, Magona's first novel, which was published on the five-year anniversary of Amy Biehl's death, was embraced by critics. For example, Jennifer Hunt comments in *American Visions*, "Eloquence is deepened by pathos as Mandisa describes the legacy that the apartheid system has bestowed upon her family and upon all black South Africans." Kai Easton was equally complimentary, claiming in the *World Literature Today*, that this novel is "Magona writing at her best."

Critics continued to praise Magona for her brave and honest work addressing social issues in South Africa. Along with critical acclaim, her writing has been honored with awards in America and South Africa. For example, her novel *Beauty's Gift*, which addressed the issue of AIDS, was on the short list for the 2009 Commonwealth Writers' Prize.

What Do I Read Next?

- Written in 2010, *The Other Half of Life* explores anti-Semitism—that is, prejudice against Jewish people. Based on the history of the MS *St. Louis*, a ship attempting to transport Jewish refugees from Nazi Germany, Kim Ablon Whitney's young-adult novel is a story of racism, loss, and hope.

- Walter Dean Meyers's *Shooter* is a young-adult novel that examines the circumstances surrounding a school shooting. Published in 2005, the story focuses on the impact that racism and bullying have on the shooter and the community.

- The second edition of Nancy L. Clark and William H. Worger's *South Africa: The Rise and Fall of Apartheid* details apartheid from 1948 to the 1990s. Published in 2011, the text includes information on South African politics in the twenty-first century.

- Nadine Gordimer's novel *July's People* was published in 1989, before the end of apartheid. In this fictional account, the apartheid government is overthrown and racial roles are reversed in South Africa, exposing the racial tension entering the 1990s.

- *To My Children's Children*, Sindiwe Magona's first book, was published in 1994. This autobiographical account of her life in South Africa showcases her personal struggles and provides a glimpse into what it was like to live under apartheid.

- *A Long Walk to Freedom* is Nelson Mandela's autobiography. Published in 2000, the book is a careful self-examination of a life spent fighting against the injustice of apartheid.

- Martin Merideth's Diamonds, *Gold, and War: The British, the Boers, and the Making of South Africa* is a nonfiction account of British colonialism and mining in South Africa. Published in 2008, the book reveals the relationship between European settlers and the native peoples.

- *A History of South Africa*, by Leonard Thompson, is a history book that begins with the country's original inhabitants and ends with Nelson Mandela and Thabo Mbeki. Published in 2001, this book is a useful overview for students interested in researching the complex history of South Africa.

Sources

"Apartheid Legislation 1850s–1970s," in *South African History Online*, http://www.sahistory.org.za/politics-and-society/apartheid-legislation-1850s-1970s (accessed August 10, 2012).

Burns, Ann, Review of *Forced to Grow*, in *Library Journal*, Vol. 123, No. 5, March 15, 1998, p. 78.

"Crime Report 2010/2011," in *South Africa Government Online*, http://www.info.gov.za/view/DownloadFileAction?id=150105 (accessed August 10, 2012).

Easton, Kai, Review of *Mother to Mother*, in *World Literature Today*, Vol. 76, No. 1, Winter 2002, pp. 124–25.

Harmon, William, *A Handbook to Literature*, 9th ed., Prentice Hall, 2003, pp. 113, 188, 210.

Hunt, Jennifer, Review of *Mother to Mother*, in *American Visions*, Vol. 15, No. 1, February–March 2000, pp. 36–37.

Magona, Sindiwe, *Mother to Mother*, Beacon Press, 1999.

———, *Forced to Grow*, Interlink Books, 1992, p. 13.

Magona, Sindiwe, Siphokazi Koyana, and Rosemary Gray, "An Electronic Interview with Sindiwe Magona," in *English in Africa*, Vol. 29,

No. 1, May 2002, pp. 99–107.

McHaney, Pearl Amelia, "History and Intertextuality: A Transnational Reading of Eudora Welty's *Losing Battles* and Sindiwe Magona's *Mother to Mother*," in *Southern Literary Journal*, Vol. 40, No. 2, Spring 2008, pp. 166–81.

"Racism," Anti-Defamation League website, http://www.adl.org/hate-patrol/racism.asp (accessed August 10, 2012).

Review of *To My Children's Children*, in *Publisher's Weekly*, May 1994, http://www.publishersweekly.com/978-1-56656-152-5 (accessed August 1, 2012).

"Sindiwe Magona," in *South African History Online*, http://www.sahistory.org.za/people/sindiwe-magona (accessed August 10, 2012).

Skelcher, Bradley, "Apartheid and the Removal of Black Spots from Lake Bhangazi in Kwazulu-Natal, South Africa," in *Journal of Black Studies*, Vol. 33, No. 6, July 2003, pp. 761–83.

"South Africa," in *CIA: The World Fact Book*, https://www.cia.gov/library/publications/the-world-factbook/geos/sf.html (accessed August 10, 2012).

"South African History: Colonial Expansion," SouthAfrica.info, http://www.southafrica.info/about/history/521102.ht (accessed August 10, 2012).

"South African History: The Death of Apartheid," SouthAfrica.info, http://www.southafrica.info/about/history/521109.ht

(accessed August 10, 2012).

Further Reading

Allen, John, *Apartheid South Africa: An Insider's Overview of the Origin and Effects of Separate Development*, iUniverse, 2005.

> Born in England and raised in South Africa, Allen includes personal experiences and South African history to bring an understanding of apartheid. He examines the motives behind apartheid and how it ultimately affected the country.

Magona, Sindiwe, Beauty's *Gift*, NB Publishers, 2011.

> This novel is a touching story that addresses AIDS in South Africa. Here, Magona shows that social action needs to continue in South Africa after the end of apartheid.

Mathabane, Mark, *Kaffir Boy: The True Story of a Black Youth's Coming of Age in Apartheid South Africa*, Scribner, 1986.

> Recommended for young-adult readers, this autobiography is an honest account of childhood in a ghetto during apartheid. Mathabane's story shows how difficult it was to escape government oppression in South Africa.

Ngcobo, Lauretta, *And They Didn't Die*, Feminist Press, 1999.

> Ngcobo's novel exposes the effect of apartheid on rural families and communities. She was a contemporary of Magona, and anyone interested in South African literature will appreciate her work.

Welsh, David, *The Rise and Fall of Apartheid*, University of Virginia Press, 2010.

> This insightful history book focuses on the beginning of apartheid and the subsequent struggles for liberation. It is a useful tool for anyone interested in the political landscape of South Africa.

Worden, Nigel, *The Making of Modern South Africa: Conquest, Apartheid, Democracy*, 5th ed., Wiley-Blackwell, 2012.

> Worden provides a comprehensive history of South Africa beginning with European settlement. The text includes updated information on the struggles the nation faced after apartheid.

Suggested Search Terms

Sindiwe Magona

Sindiwe Magona AND biography

Mother to Mother AND Sindiwe Magona

Sindiwe Magona AND criticism

Mother to Mother AND Amy Biehl apartheid

South Africa AND history

South Africa AND settlement

Mother to Mother AND review

CPSIA information can be obtained
at www.ICGtesting.com
Printed in the USA
BVHW041641120321
602399BV00009B/572

9 781375 384643